Speak Logically 1

SPEECH TOPICS for KIDS

saramin

Introduction

Speak Logically: SPEECH TOPICS for KIDS was designed to teach young students the basic elements of public speaking and to prepare them to become confident English speakers. Students develop their speeches through vocabulary, listening, organizing, and speech writing exercises. Each unit includes a model speech and public speaking tips. Through regular practice and presentations, students improve public speaking skills and overall fluency.

Table of Contents

Unit Breakdown

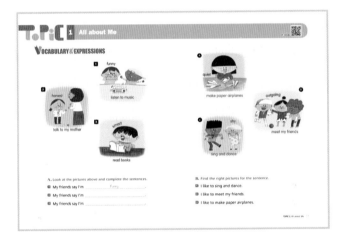

Introduce T.PiC

Students are presented with a new topic in each unit. They share personal experiences and opinions on a given topic with classmates through warm up questions and class discussions.

WHAT TO DO:

1. Ask one or two warm up questions to get students thinking about their personal experiences about the topic.
2. Have a brief classroom discussion to see how much students know and how well they are able to express themselves about the given topic.

VOCABULARY & EXPRESSIONS MP3

Students learn words and expressions related to the speech topic. The audio file allows them to listen to and practice the correct pronunciation of each word and expression.

WHAT TO DO:

1 Listen to vocabulary words on audio.
2 Go over any unfamiliar words, offer words with similar meanings, and provide more examples.
3 Ask students to come up with more words related to the speech topic.
4 Add the new words to the vocabulary list for future reference.

Students complete spelling, vocabulary, and grammar exercises in preparation for speech writing. Vocabulary Practice helps students become familiar with new vocabulary and see how it is used in a sentence.

WHAT TO DO:

1 Have students complete exercises and then take up answers.
2 Answers can be taken up as a class or in pairs.
  (Answers provided in Teachers' Guide.)

LISTENING PRACTICE MP3

Students are presented with a dialog between two to three people. They listen to the dialog and answer questions. When put in order, the answers become the model speech presented in the following section of the unit. In addition, Listening Practice demonstrates the logical sequence of the model speech: *Introductory statement – Reason - Example/Details - Closing Statement.*

WHAT TO DO:

1 Listen to the dialog and have students write out answers in full.

2 Listen to the dialog again so students can double check their answers.

3 Take up answers. (Answers provided in Teachers' Guide.)

MODEL SPEECH MP3

Students listen to a model speech and then practice reading the speech out loud alone or to a partner. They focus on pronouncing the words and listening to themselves speak. The model speech gives students an example of how a speech is written using words from the vocabulary list and how it sounds when spoken at the average speaking rate in a strong, confident voice.

WHAT TO DO:

1 Listen to the model speech.

2 Have students read it out loud three times either alone or in pairs.

BRAINSTORM

Students are presented with questions and/or graphic organizers. They learn to gather and organize information in preparation for speech writing. Students are encouraged to use vocabulary and expressions learned in the unit.

WHAT TO DO:

1 Read over questions, explain in detail what to do.

2 Have students fill in the graphic organizer and write out their answers.

3 If time permits, have students share their ideas with a partner.

SPEECH  WRITING

Students personalize a speech by filling in the blanks with information from their brainstorm. Each student completes their speech to practice and present to the class.

WHAT TO DO:

1 Have students fill in the blanks using information gathered in their brainstorm.

2 Once speeches are completed, they should look over their writing for any spelling or grammatical errors.

3 If time permits, have students work in pairs to read each other's speeches and check for any mistakes.

PRESENTATION

The Presentation section is divided into three sections. In section A, students write out their entire speech. In section B, students record their speeches and practice in front of a mirror. Students also practice a new public speaking skill in each unit such as using body language and their voices correctly. In section C, students complete a chart after presenting their speeches. The focus is on learning, practicing, and improving basic public speaking skills through each presentation, not on how perfectly each speech is delivered.

WHAT TO DO:

BEFORE PRESENTATIONS:

1 Have students write out the full speech.
2 Go over the steps to follow when practicing and give adequate time for practice.
3 Introduce the public speaking tip included in the Teachers' Guide.
4 If time permits, break the class into smaller groups or pairs for more practice.
5 Before starting presentations, go over any unfamiliar words in section C.

DURING PRESENTATIONS:

1 Make sure all students give their full attention to each speaker.
2 The goal is to have students thinking and speaking at the same time with minimal assistance. Students should be discouraged from using cue cards or reading their speeches from their textbooks. If a student gets stuck while presenting, provide a few words from their speech as hints so they can pick up from where they left off.

AFTER PRESENTATIONS:

1 Provide brief feedback and words of encouragement for each student immediately after his presentation. Feedback is most effective when given right after a

presentation as it will be fresh in the student's mind.

2 Classmates may also provide feedback to the presenter. Ask the class, "What is something the speaker did very well?", "What did you like about his speech?" Getting the class involved will encourage them to listen and watch their peers' presentations more attentively.

3 Each student should complete Section C immediately after their presentation.

⊕ ADDITIONAL SUGGESTIONS

Set up a video camera in class to record students during presentations. Students get the chance to see what they look and sound like in front of an audience. It will also help them identify their strengths and weaknesses which they can further work on for the next presentation. Videos also help students feel more comfortable speaking in front of a camera. It may be fun for students to watch themselves on a classroom Youtube channel and to leave positive feedback for each other.

VOCABULARY & EXPRESSIONS

1 funny

listen to music

2 honest

talk to my mother

3 smart

read books

A. Look at the pictures above and complete the sentences.

1 My friends say I'm _____funny_____.

2 My friends say I'm _____.

3 My friends say I'm _____.

quiet

make paper airplanes

outgoing

meet my friends

shy

sing and dance

B. Find the right pictures for the sentence.

1 I like to sing and dance.

2 I like to meet my friends.

3 I like to make paper airplanes.

 **ISTENING PRACTICE**

01_02

Listen and answer the questions using the sentences below.

> I like to read books.
>
> Hi, my name is Mindy!
>
> My friends say I'm funny.

1 What is your name?

_____

2 What do you like to do?

_____

3 What do your friends say about you?

_____

4 Nice to meet you all!

MODEL SPEECH

Listen to the speech and then read it out loud three times.

Hi, my name is Mindy.

I like to read books.

My friends say I'm funny.

Nice to meet you all!

BRAINSTORM

Make a list of words and expressions that describe you.

1. What do you like to do?

2. What do your friends say about you?

SPEECH WRITING

Use the words from your brainstorm to fill in the blanks.

Hi, my name is _____ .

I like to _____ .

My friends say I'm _____ .

Nice to meet you all!

RESENTATION

A Write your entire speech below.

⦿ Record

_____

_____

_____

_____

_____

_____

_____

B Practice your speech in the following steps:

STEP **1** Read your speech out loud.

STEP **2** Record your voice and listen to your speech.

STEP **3** Stand in front of a mirror and say your speech 3 times.
Try to remember the main points.

PRACTICE Out Loud!

C Present your speech and answer the questions below.

CRITERIA	Yes	No
1 Did I stand straight and tall?		
2 Did I speak loudly enough?		
3 Did I make eye contact with the audience?		

VOCABULARY & EXPRESSIONS

1

healthy

riding bicycles

2

creative

drawing pictures

3

fun

watching movies

A. Draw a line between each hobby and the matching word.

1 riding bicycles •   • creative

2 drawing pictures •   • fun

3 watching movies •   • healthy

A

exciting

collecting trading cards

B

relaxing

taking care of my pet

C

interesting

reading books

B. Look at the pictures above and complete each sentence.

A My hobby is ___collecting trading cards___ .

B My hobby is _____ .

C My hobby is _____ .

 **ISTENING PRACTICE**

Listen and answer the questions using the sentences below.

> It's a healthy hobby because I get a lot of exercise.
>
> My hobby is riding bicycles.
>
> I ride my bicycle three times a week.

1 What is your hobby?

_____

2 How often do you ride your bicycle?

_____

3 What word best describes your hobby and why?

_____

4 You should try it too!

MODEL SPEECH

02_03

Listen to the speech and then read it out loud three times.

My hobby is riding bicycles.

I ride my bicycle three times a week.

It's a healthy hobby because I get a lot of exercise.

You should try it too!

PRACTICE
Out Loud!

1
2
3

BRAINSTORM

Answer questions about your hobby.

1. What are your hobbies?	2. Which one do you like best?

3. How often do you do your hobby?
   Circle one answer or write your own.

   ⓐ every day　　ⓑ once a week　　ⓒ 3 times a week
   ⓓ 1-2 times a month　　ⓔ _____

4. What word best describes your hobby? Why?

SPEECH WRITING

Use the words from your brainstorm to fill in the blanks.

My hobby is _____ .

I _____ .

It's a _____ hobby

because _____ .

You should try it too!

RESENTATION

A Write your entire speech below.

⦿ Record

_____

_____

_____

_____

_____

_____

_____

_____

_____

_____

B Practice your speech in the following steps:

STEP **1** Read your speech out loud.

STEP **2** Record your voice and listen to your speech.

STEP **3** Stand in front of a mirror and say your speech 3 times.
Try to remember the main points.

PRACTICE
Out Loud!

C Present your speech and answer the questions below.

CRITERIA	Yes	No
1 Did I stand straight and tall?		
2 Did I speak loudly enough?		
3 Did I make eye contact with the audience?		

T.PiC 3 Food

VOCABULARY & EXPRESSIONS

2

salty

fried rice

1

sweet

chocolate

3

crunchy

French fries

A. Look at the pictures above and complete each sentence.

1 _____Chocolate_____ is my favorite food.

2 _____ is my favorite food.

3 _____ are my favorite food.

chewy

spaghetti

spicy

instant noodles

juicy

watermelon

B. Draw a line between the food and its taste.

1 instant noodles   •

  • juicy

2 spaghetti   •

  • chewy

3 watermelon   •

  • spicy

 **ISTENING PRACTICE**

Listen and answer the questions using the sentences below.

> They taste delicious with ketchup.
>
> French fries are my favorite food.
>
> I love French fries because they are salty and crunchy.

1 What is your favorite food?

_____

2 Why do you like them so much?

_____

3 What do they taste good with?

_____

4 I could eat French fries every day!

03_03

Listen to the speech and then read it out loud three times.

French fries are my favorite food.

I love French fries because they are salty and crunchy.

They taste delicious with ketchup.

I could eat French fries every day!

PRACTICE
Out Loud!
1
2
3

BRAINSTORM

Write one word in each box that describes your favorite food.

taste

color

My favorite food:
_____

smell

SPEECH WRITING

Use the words from your brainstorm to fill in the blanks.

[   ] is/are my favorite food.

I love [   ] because it is/they are

[   ] and [   ].

It/They taste(s) delicious with [   ].

I could eat [   ] every day!

PRESENTATION

A **Write your entire speech below.** ⊙ Record

_____

_____

_____

_____

_____

_____

_____

_____

B **Practice your speech in the following steps:**

STEP **1** Read your speech out loud.

STEP **2** Record your voice and listen to your speech.

STEP **3** Stand in front of a mirror and say your speech 3 times.
Try to remember the main points.

PRACTICE
Out Loud!

C **Present your speech and answer the questions below.**

CRITERIA	Yes	No
1 Did I stand straight and tall?		
2 Did I speak loudly enough?		
3 Did I make eye contact with the audience?		

VOCABULARY & EXPRESSIONS

strong
elephant

fierce
shark

soft
hamster

fast
lion

hairy
monkey

friendly
dog

lazy
panda

tall
giraffe

A. Write the singular and plural form of each animal.

1

 →

elephant   elephants

2

 →

3

 →

B. Complete the sentences.

1 Elephants are _____ strong _____ .

2 Sharks are _____ .

3 Dogs are _____ .

 **ISTENING PRACTICE**

04_02

Listen and answer the questions using the sentences below.

> They are big and grey.
>
> I like elephants because they are strong.
>
> Elephants are my favorite animal.

1 What is your favorite animal?

_____

2 What do they look like?

_____

3 Why do you like them?

_____

4 Elephants are the best!

MODEL SPEECH

04_03

Listen to the speech and then read it out loud three times.

Elephants are my favorite animal.

They are big and grey.

I like elephants because they are strong.

Elephants are the best!

PRACTICE
Out Loud!
1
2
3

BRAINSTORM

Write a word in each box that describes your favorite animal.

My favorite animal:

_____

SPEECH WRITING

Use the words from your brainstorm to fill in the blanks.

_____ are my favorite animal.

They are _____ and _____ .

I like _____ because they are

_____ .

_____ are the best!

RESENTATION

A Write your entire speech below.   ⦿ Record

_____

_____

_____

_____

_____

_____

_____

B Practice your speech in the following steps:

STEP **1** Read your speech out loud.

STEP **2** Record your voice and listen to your speech.

STEP **3** Stand in front of a mirror and say your speech 3 times.
Try to remember the main points.

PRACTICE
Out Loud!

C Present your speech and answer the questions below.

CRITERIA	Yes	No
1 Did I stand straight and tall?		
2 Did I speak loudly enough?		
3 Did I make eye contact with the audience?		

VOCABULARY & EXPRESSIONS

Sunday	Monday	Tuesday	Wednesday	Thursday	Friday	Saturday
			1	2	3	4 take a long nap
5	6	7	8 go to the park	9	10	11
12	13	14	15	16 learn the guitar	17	18
19	20	21 play games with friends	22	23	24	25
26 visit my grandparents	27	28	29	30		

A. Write the days of a week in the correct order.

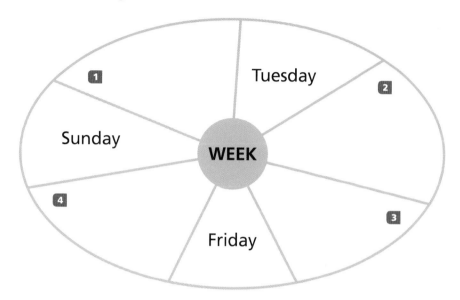

B. Complete each sentence.

 **LISTENING PRACTICE**

05_02

Listen and answer the questions using the sentences below.

> I visit my grandmother's home.
>
> My favorite day of the week is Friday.
>
> I eat delicious food and take a long nap.

1 What is your favorite day of the week?

_____

2 What do you usually do on this day?

_____

3 What do you do there?

_____

4 I wish every day was Friday!

MODEL SPEECH

05_03

Listen to the speech and then read it out loud three times.

My favorite day of the week is Friday.

I visit my grandmother's home.

I eat delicious food and take a long nap.

I wish every day was Friday!

PRACTICE
Out Loud!

BRAINSTORM

Write a word in each box that describes your favorite day.

What do you usually do on this day?

My favorite
day of the week:

SPEECH WRITING

Use the words from your brainstorm to fill in the blanks.

My favorite day of the week is _____ .

I _____ .

I _____ .

I wish every day was _____ !

RESENTATION

A Write your entire speech below.

◉ Record

_____

_____

_____

_____

_____

_____

_____

B Practice your speech in the following steps:

STEP **1** Read your speech out loud.

STEP **2** Record your voice and listen to your speech.

STEP **3** Stand in front of a mirror and say your speech 3 times. Try to remember the main points.

PRACTICE
Out Loud!
1
2
3

C Present your speech and answer the questions below.

CRITERIA	Yes	No
1 Did I stand straight and tall?		
2 Did I speak loudly enough?		
3 Did I make eye contact with the audience?		

VOCABULARY & EXPRESSIONS

good at computer games

good at dancing

good at sports

A. Look at the pictures above and complete each sentence.

1 She is good at ___computer games___ .

2 He is good at _____ .

3 He is good at _____ .

B. Look at the pictures above and complete each sentence.

A Jane likes to go camping. She is _adventurous_ .

B Gio shares his umbrella with a dog. He is _____ .

C Sam is good at playing the cello. He is _____ .

 **ISTENING PRACTICE**

🔊 06_02

Listen and answer the questions using the sentences below.

> Jenny is good at singing and dancing.
>
> We have been friends for three years.
>
> My best friend, Jenny is talented.

1 How would you describe your best friend?

_____

2 What is your best friend good at?

_____

3 How long have you been friends?

_____

4 I hope we stay best friends forever.

MODEL SPEECH

 06_03

Listen to the speech and then read it out loud three times.

My best friend, Jenny is talented.

Jenny is good at singing and dancing.

We have been friends for three years.

I hope we stay best friends forever.

PRACTICE
Out Loud!

BRAINSTORM

Answer questions about your best friend.

1. Who is your best friend?

2. How would you describe your best friend?

3. What is your best friend good at?

4. How long have you been friends? Circle one answer or write your own.

   (a) 6 months   (b) 1 year   (c) 2 years   (d) 3 years

   (e) _____

SPEECH WRITING

Use the words from your brainstorm to fill in the blanks.

My best friend _____ is _____ .

_____ is good at _____ and _____ .

We have been friends for _____ .

I hope we stay best friends forever.

RESENTATION

A **Write your entire speech below.** ⦿ Record

....

....

....

....

....

....

....

B **Practice your speech in the following steps:**

STEP **1** Read your speech out loud.

STEP **2** Record your voice and listen to your speech.

STEP **3** Stand in front of a mirror and say your speech 3 times.
Try to remember the main points.

PRACTICE
Out Loud!

C **Present your speech and answer the questions below.**

CRITERIA	Yes	No
1 Did I stand straight and tall?		
2 Did I speak loudly enough?		
3 Did I make eye contact with the audience?		

VOCABULARY & EXPRESSIONS

nice

blue

beautiful

red

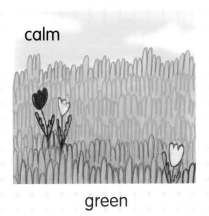

calm

green

excited

orange

relaxed

purple

energetic

yellow

A. Complete each sentence.

1 _____ is the nicest color.

2 _____ is the nicest color.

3 _____ is the nicest color.

B. Draw a line between each sentence and the correct picture.

1 Red makes me feel **beautiful**.   •   •

2 Green makes me feel **calm**.   •   •

3 Yellow makes me feel **energetic**.   •   •

Listen and answer the questions using the sentences below.

> It makes me feel energetic.
>
> Yellow is the nicest color.
>
> I like yellow fruit such as bananas and pineapples.

1 In your opinion, what is the nicest color?

_____

2 How does it make you feel?

_____

3 What objects or food of this color do you like?

_____

4 That is why yellow is my favorite color.

MODEL SPEECH

Listen to the speech and then read it out loud three times.

Yellow is the nicest color.

It makes me feel energetic.

I like yellow fruit such as bananas and pineapples.

That is why yellow is my favorite color.

PRACTICE
Out Loud!

BRAINSTORM

Answer questions about your favorite color.

1. Circle your favorite color.

red	blue	pink	green	yellow
purple	orange	brown	gold	silver
black	white	sky blue		

2. How does your favorite color make you feel?

3. What objects or food of this color do you like?

SPEECH WRITING

Use the words from your brainstorm to fill in the blanks.

_____ is the nicest color.

It makes me feel _____ .

I like _____ .

That is why _____ is my favorite color.

RESENTATION

A Write your entire speech below.

◉ Record

_____

_____

_____

_____

_____

_____

_____

B Practice your speech in the following steps:

STEP **1** Read your speech out loud.

STEP **2** Record your voice and listen to your speech.

STEP **3** Stand in front of a mirror and say your speech 3 times.
Try to remember the main points.

PRACTICE
Out Loud!

C Present your speech and answer the questions below.

CRITERIA	Yes	No
1 Did I stand straight and tall?		
2 Did I speak loudly enough?		
3 Did I make eye contact with the audience?		

T.PiC

VOCABULARY & EXPRESSIONS

visit museums

help me with my
homework

play board games

father

mother

me

older brother

younger sister

help me clean
my room

cook dinner

watch movies

A. Match each word with the opposite meaning.

1. girl •   • father

2. older •   • sister

3. brother •   • younger

4. mother •   • boy

B. Look at the pictures and complete each sentence.

1. My family likes to _____ together.

2. My family likes to _____ together.

3. My family likes to _____ together.

 **ISTENING PRACTICE**

08_02

Listen and answer the questions using the sentences below.

> My mother and father are kind.
>
> There are four people in my family.
>
> My family likes to visit museums together.
>
> My older sister helps me with my homework.

1 How many people are there in your family?

_____

2 How would you describe your mother and father?

_____

3 What do your parents or sibling(s) help you with?

_____

4 What does your family like to do together?

_____

MODEL SPEECH

08_03

Listen to the speech and then read it out loud three times.

There are four people in my family.

My mother and father are kind.

My older sister helps me with my homework.

My family likes to visit museums together.

PRACTICE
Out Loud!
1
2
3

BRAINSTORM

Answer questions about your family.

1. How many people are there in your family?

2. How would you describe your mother and father?

3. What do your parents or sibling(s) help you with?

4. What does your family like to do together?

SPEECH WRITING

Use the words from your brainstorm to fill in the blanks.

There are _____ people in my family.

My mother and father are _____ .

My _____ help(s) me _____ .

My family likes to _____ together.

RESENTATION

A **Write your entire speech below.** ◉ Record

_____

_____

_____

_____

_____

_____

_____

B **Practice your speech in the following steps:**

STEP **1** Read your speech out loud.

STEP **2** Record your voice and listen to your speech.

STEP **3** Stand in front of a mirror and say your speech 3 times.
Try to remember the main points.

PRACTICE
Out Loud!

C **Present your speech and answer the questions below.**

CRITERIA	Yes	No
1 Did I stand straight and tall?		
2 Did I speak loudly enough?		
3 Did I make eye contact with the audience?		

VOCABULARY & EXPRESSIONS

A. Complete each sentence.

1

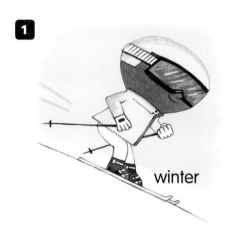

winter

It's _____.

2

summer

It's _____.

3

spring

It's _____.

4

fall

It's _____.

eat - ate

go - went

see - saw

B. Write the past tense of each verb two times.

Present   Past

A eat   ➡   _____   _____

B go   ➡   _____   _____

C see   ➡   _____   _____

 **ISTENING PRACTICE** 📓 09_02

Listen and answer the questions using the sentences below.

> We traveled to Jeju Island.
>
> Last summer, I went on a vacation with my family.
>
> We swam and ate a lot of delicious seafood.
>
> We got there by airplane.

1 When was your most recent vacation?

_____

2 Where did you go?

_____

3 How did you get there?

_____

4 What are two things you did there?

_____

MODEL SPEECH

09_03

Listen to the speech and then read it out loud three times.

Last summer, I went on a vacation with my family.

We traveled to Jeju Island.

We got there by airplane.

We swam and ate a lot of delicious seafood.

PRACTICE Out Loud!

BRAINSTORM

Think about your most recent vacation and answer the questions below.

1. WHEN? (When was your vacation?)	
2. WHO? (Who did you travel with?)	
3. WHERE? (Where did you go?)	
4. HOW? (How did you get there?)	
5. WHAT (What are two things you did there?)	

SPEECH WRITING

Use the words from your brainstorm to fill in the blanks.

Last _____, I went on a vacation with _____.

We traveled to _____.

We got there by _____.

We _____ and _____.

PRESENTATION

A Write your entire speech below.

◉ Record

_____

_____

_____

_____

_____

_____

_____

_____

B Practice your speech in the following steps:

STEP **1** Read your speech out loud.

STEP **2** Record your voice and listen to your speech.

STEP **3** Stand in front of a mirror and say your speech 3 times. Try to remember the main points.

PRACTICE Out Loud!

C Present your speech and answer the questions below.

CRITERIA	Yes	No
1 Did I stand straight and tall?		
2 Did I speak loudly enough?		
3 Did I make eye contact with the audience?		

VOCABULARY & EXPRESSIONS

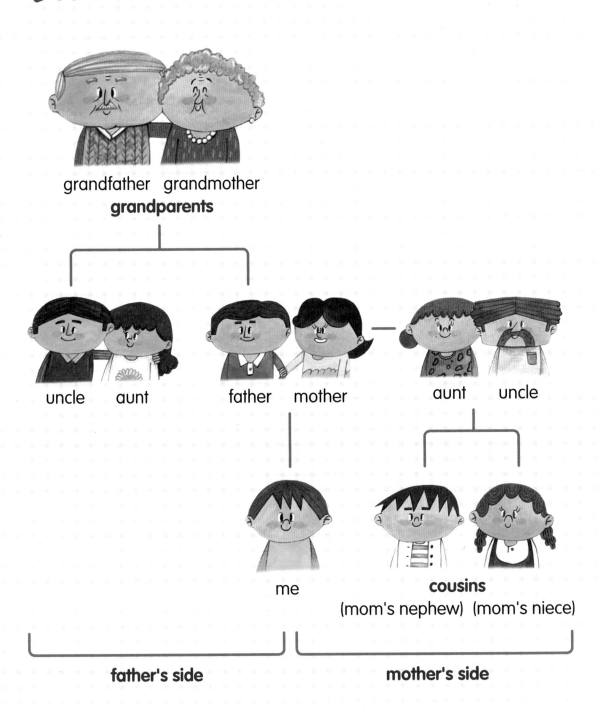

grandfather   grandmother
grandparents

uncle   aunt   father   mother   aunt   uncle

me   **cousins**
(mom's nephew) (mom's niece)

father's side   **mother's side**

A. Match each word with the correct explanation.

1 grandfather •   • father or mother's sister

2 cousin •   • father or mother's brother

3 uncle •   • uncle or aunt's son

4 aunt •   • father or mother's father

B. Look at the family tree (p.64) and complete each sentence.

1 I have _____ cousins.

2 I have _____ uncles and _____ aunts.

3 My father has _____ brother(s).

 **ISTENING PRACTICE** 10_02

Listen and answer the questions using the sentences below.

> I have many relatives.
>
> My favorite relative is my aunt because she is a very good cook.
>
> I have 2 grandmothers, 3 aunts, 3 uncles, and 4 cousins.

1 Do you have many relatives?

_____

2 How many relatives do you have?

_____

3 Who is your favorite relative?

_____

4 I wish I could see her more often.

MODEL SPEECH

Listen to the speech and then read it out loud three times.

I have many relatives.

I have 2 grandmothers, 3 aunts, 3 uncles, and 4 cousins.

My favorite relative is my aunt because she is a very good cook.

PRACTICE
Out Loud!
1
2
3

I wish I could see her more often.

BRAINSTORM

Create a family tree.

Father's side

Grandfather	Grandmother

Mother's side

Grandfather	Grandfather

My dad

My mom

me

1. Do you have many relatives?

2. Who is your favorite relative?

3. Why is he/she your favorite relative?

SPEECH WRITING

Use the information from your brainstorm to fill in the blanks.

I have/don't have many relatives.

I have _____.

My favorite relative is my _____ because

_____.

I wish I could see _____ more often.

RESENTATION

A **Write your entire speech below.**

⊙ Record

_____

_____

_____

_____

_____

_____

_____

_____

_____

_____

B **Practice your speech in the following steps:**

STEP **1** Read your speech out loud.

STEP **2** Record your voice and listen to your speech.

STEP **3** Stand in front of a mirror and say your speech 3 times.
Try to remember the main points.

PRACTICE
Out Loud!

C **Present your speech and answer the questions below.**

CRITERIA	Yes	No
1 Did I stand straight and tall?		
2 Did I speak loudly enough?		
3 Did I make eye contact with the audience?		

VOCABULARY & EXPRESSIONS

Complete each sentence.

1

I want to be a _____ .

doctor

athlete

2

I want to be an _____ .

3

I want to be a _____ .

computer programmer

11_01

actor

4

I want to be an _____.

police
officer

5

I want to be a _____.

chef

6

I want to be a _____.

TOPIC 11. Future Jobs 75

 **ISTENING PRACTICE** 11_02

Listen and answer the questions using the sentences below.

> I want to help others and catch bad people.
>
> When I grow up, I want to be a police officer.
>
> A police officer must be clever and brave.

1 What do you want to be when you grow up?

_____

2 Why do you want this job?

_____

3 What two qualities must a police officer have?

_____

4 I will become the best police officer!

MODEL SPEECH

11_03

Listen to the speech and then read it out loud three times.

When I grow up, I want to be a police officer.

I want to help others and catch bad people.

A police officer must be clever and brave.

I will become the best police officer!

PRACTICE
Out Loud!

1
2
3

BRAINSTORM

Answer questions about the job you want to have in the future.

1. What do you want to be when you grow up?

2. Why do you want this job?

3. What two qualities must you have for this job?
   Circle two answers or write your own.

   (a) brave   (b) clever   (c) creative

   (d) hard working   (e) intelligent   (f) outgoing

   (g) patient   (h) _____

SPEECH WRITING

Use the words from your brainstorm to fill in the blanks.

When I grow up, I want to be [a/an] [   ] .

I want to [   ] .

[A/An] [   ] must be [   ]

and [   ] .

I will become the best [   ] !

78

RESENTATION

A Write your entire speech below.

◉ Record

_____

_____

_____

_____

_____

_____

_____

_____

B Practice your speech in the following steps:

STEP **1** Read your speech out loud.

STEP **2** Record your voice and listen to your speech.

STEP **3** Stand in front of a mirror and say your speech 3 times.
Try to remember the main points.

PRACTICE
Out Loud!

C Present your speech and answer the questions below.

CRITERIA	Yes	No
1 Did I stand straight and tall?		
2 Did I speak loudly enough?		
3 Did I make eye contact with the audience?		

12 Movies

VOCABULARY & EXPRESSIONS

Complete each sentence.

1

I enjoy watching _____ movies.

comedy

action

2

I enjoy watching _____ movies.

3

I enjoy watching _____ movies.

mystery

horror

4

I enjoy watching _____ movies.

fantasy

5

I enjoy watching _____ movies.

animation

6

I enjoy watching _____ movies.

superhero

7

I enjoy watching _____ movies.

 **ISTENING PRACTICE** 🔊 12_02

Listen and answer the questions using the sentences below.

> The character I like most is Woody because he is cute.
>
> I enjoy watching animation movies.
>
> I give the movie 5 stars.
>
> My favorite movie is *Toy Story*.

1 What kind of movies do you like?

_____

2 What is your favorite movie?

_____

3 Which character do you like most? Why?

_____

4 How many stars would you give the movie?

_____

MODEL SPEECH

 12_03

Listen to the speech and then read it out loud three times.

I enjoy watching animation movies.

My favorite movie is *Toy Story*.

The character I like most is Woody because he is cute.

I give the movie 5 stars.

PRACTICE
Out Loud!
1
2
3

BRAINSTORM

Answer questions about your favorite movie.

1. What kind of movies do you like?

2. What is your favorite movie?

3. Which character do you like most? Why?

4. How many stars would you give this movie?

   poor ☆ ☆ ☆ ☆ ☆ good

SPEECH WRITING

Use the words from your brainstorm to fill in the blanks.

I enjoy watching [   ] movies.

My favorite movie is [   ].

The character I like most is [   ]

because he/she [   ].

I give the movie [   ] star(s).

84

PRESENTATION

A Write your entire speech below.

⦿ Record

_____

_____

_____

_____

_____

_____

_____

B Practice your speech in the following steps:

STEP **1** Read your speech out loud.

STEP **2** Record your voice and listen to your speech.

PRACTICE
Out Loud!

STEP **3** Stand in front of a mirror and say your speech 3 times.
Try to remember the main points.

C Present your speech and answer the questions below.

CRITERIA	Yes	No
1 Did I stand straight and tall?		
2 Did I speak loudly enough?		
3 Did I make eye contact with the audience?